I0098103

50 POEMS IN A DAY

CHANNELING DELIVERANCE

THROUGH POETRY

By

Anthony Brown

STREAMING CONSCIOUSNESS

1

In the middle of the night

My mind takes flight

Into a world owned by imagination and glory

Wanting to tell its own story

Absent the pain of life's daily stream

Of bad news, impending deadlines

Time to dream…of a better tomorrow

A more fulfilling today

A less earth shattering yesterday

In the recess…of my heart's divine purpose

Lies an enigma

A mystery in time's suspension

I don't understand why my life has to be this way

Direct me…wanting your warmth and Spirit

Have any ideas on a firm direction to life's Source?

Whatever your name is, I have no remorse

In loving you

THE MAN IN THE MIRROR

2

I'm looking

But see nothing

Tasting

But not sensing the recipe

Biting

But no grip on reality

Spitting…out society's way of thinking

Standing in the truth of my life's shine

With no hesitation or blinking

I have meaning

My life's direction should spell it out

But with every step a new adventure…clouds reason

And spins my wheels turning once again

Give me time

But what is time's ETA

Give me Love

But once present how long can Love stay

I love you

But does that love's expression hold your gaze?

VICTORY OR DEATH

3

Give me victory or give me death

Seems boring right now

Tell me something with more heft

Life interests me

Death is an appointment whose time isn't set

Love the way you lie

Sounds more like denial then a Grammy nominated tune

Maybe I'll just look into the sky

The birds have got it down

No rent money due

Their wings respond to freedom's wind

Follow the birds Flight

And to this life's folly say good night

BOLD AND BEAUTIFUL

4

I'M GOING TO DELIVER SOMEONE...

To the knowledge of a broken me

I'm scared

My clear eyes can barely see

The foundation of a trust unsure

My confusion clouds every path

But my direction's call feels so near

Do what you must

Have an imperative

Have a law for the love you provide

For your soul's call to arms...

Violent is the soul's way of doing things

It has to travel so far to your open hands reach

To direct its movement

Good luck with that!

Why did I say that?

Why does resistance speak so loud?

Why???

Give in to Freedom

Just Give in

I CRY OUT

5

I cry out to Love

Love hears me

And answers

In the stench of my soul's disparity

 It reaches my hands' pain

Giving me a joy unspeakable

And walking my heart's fear into its embrace

I got up on that stage

Preached my guts out

Didn't even flinch

Didn't even bat an eye

My spirit, soul and body in alignment

What a natural high

I need it

Love it!

Want it

Changing my life by the love present in every human being

Giving me passion for my life's abyss

It won't let me fall in

Don't let me falter in this existence without the pain of its

purpose…I LOVE YOU!!!!!

ANCHOR

6

I need an anchor

Your love's call is a tether that reaches down deep

What's your name?

What passion steadies your mind oh Lord

You are past fathoming

Your hand so sure

I love you

I need you

I want you

I have to have your call's discipline

Your blood's name

Transfer me out of this world's reality

Into a different time and space I can call home

THE LOVE OF WHO YOU ARE

7

I fall in love with you every day

Every crinkle of your nose's smile

Every saying, you make a reality

Every movement you etch into my heart's reason for being

Heels that reach the sky

A heart that carries the depth of the ocean's treasure

My name is locked up in your heart's expression and you wear it so

well

It's your bathing suit and evening dress all in one

The thought of your anger's end is even fun

I met you in the twilight of my purpose's reach

The person you met died, the real me lay beneath

You stayed for the encore

And never put me beneath your feet

Beside me, before me, in front of me

Your interest never seems to peak

I gotta say… I love you

I really need you to know I care

The peace that comes from your resonance

I'm fascinated by the way your excellence laughs

And am enthralled by the sequence of your loving action's

exercise…in creative expression

THE LOVE OF WHO YOU ARE…

Resonates with the peace in and of, who I want to be

For that I give thanks, forever

And she smiles ☺

IT'S TIME TO BELIEVE

8

Ever thought you weren't going to make it

We are all one…

How could you get lost in you?

See the truth in that

Be that truth

Live that truth

Let that truth set you free…

ONE IN A MILLION

9

Fast thought

Slow response

Build your spiritual muscles please

The world needs your gift

I need your lift

My dad loves you, didn't you know

My sisters in heaven, she lives in the heart of God's mind

Always wanted her

Always needed her perspective

Her realization is my heart's fulfillment

In my daughter's smile

Everyone is connected

Every person's dream contingent upon another soul's reality

So love others not as you want to be loved

Love others as yourself

Love them like you get hungry for your favorite salmon cooked just

right

Love people

Love people

Love people

Because when you love people

You love God's only Son, who is you

Let that sun shine on the glory of your frailty

And turn it to His greatest strength

Just be…

HATE HAS NO PLACE IN THIS DOJO

10

Karate

Kung Fu

Kangaroo kicks in Tekken 6

Karen Mitchell, my mother's slap on my disrespect's face

Man that hurt!

I woke up and realized she could still kick my ass that day

Don't be the man of a house you don't run…that's suicide bro, with

its reality don't flirt!

Just a little tip

A reality I tried to skip……….

A hateful statement…what a powerful force of wrongness

Wrapped up in a teenager's smile

What is this little shit up to this time?

He's off by a mile

I've been that…

So I know the mischief in his mind, is about to climb

Into a plan of attack that sees a righteous end…

No keys to the Stang today…because the trash stinks

Take it out Batman!

Take it out Dr. Doom!

Take the fuckin trash out…and stop talking about mine

Do your homework…I already know the meaning of life!!!

Your view is a little skewed don't ya think?…by the inward parts of

your fantasy girlfriend's perfection

Just take the fucking trash out and stop drinking all the milk in the

fridge boy

Damn!

DID I JUST SAY THAT?

11

I WANT THIS WOMAN SO BAD!!!

Time to start saying things I don't mean, from a tone I can't

maintain, in a way I can't relate to.

My bro said you was fine, I'm like "she aiight"

"Yeah well my bellies like a stone fortress of fatty pleasure baby,

you know you wanna bounce off of its radiance!"

"Don't get me wrong, I really want to hit that but I'm a little tired

today…feel me?"

"Well whoever told you that about me was way off, King Midas is a

tree trunk baby, a real body slammer, a magic hammer,

yeeeeaaahhhh!"

Then I realized I was losing her…losing her forever…losing the

heart of her soul's compassion.

So I changed it up…

"I'm really not that guy"

"Not a Cretan"

"Not your beauty's spy"

"I've seen you around"

"And a smile comes to my face after, always"

"I'd pay to see you smile"

"Because it brings me joy"

"And I'm surrounded by so much pain"

"SO CAN I HIT THAT?"

Well ladies, can he?   ☺

ARE YOU SERIOUS?

12

Are you really going to act like you didn't just blow up the spot?

The flowers are wilting…the atmosphere is full of your stench's rot

Alright I can't do it, why did I even start

Can't write a poem just about a fart

Maybe a change of heart

Is just what the doctor ordered

I think that move is smart

Don't you?

Remember when you discovered your life had meaning?

Remember when fucking became an art and not just a goal?

Remember when you saw a movie and for the first time cried

Because your life was being paraded before you so rudely…

You were undone, and a nervous laugh turned into a deep sigh

Come back to yourself

Life's not so bad that a fart should have more meaning than a child's

mended heart

Come back to your dreams

Buildings are still burning

Waiting for the perfect fireman…that was going to be you

But from the realization of that buildings call…your mind kept

turning

To the rational and sensible answer

The direction that was laid out for you from birth…

From a father who loved Chow Mein noodles

And from his restaurant's kitchen, he would always revel in the

loudest of his farts

Maybe that's why you want to right now

The influence's that drive our days purpose…

I tell you

STICKS AND STONES

13

Childhood is so close to me right now

First crushes

Girls that liked hurting you on the basketball court to let you know

how much they digged you…

Ice cream scoops that melt down the side of the cone…girls licking

the ice cream up from the side of that cone

Man I miss the simple

Accept for waking up in the morning and feeling the headache from

an adolescent pimple…

Tests…

Failing them

Passing them

Not caring either way

What do you want to be when you grow up?

A fun question at the time

As an adult a question that insinuates loser-ness

Pencils with the sharpest lead

Why did that even matter?

Titties

Ass

Big titties

Titties period…

SHAKE IT OFF

14

Yo mammas so ugly, she scared a Pitbull away from his bone

Yo daddy is so stupid that he taught you how to breathe while
holding his breath and passed out before the lesson was done

Your sister's so awkward…a giraffe came up to her and asked her if
she needed a friend

Your brothers so horny, that he saw to dogs humping and cried
because he thought they were making fun of him

Just practice…
If you don't get it then maybe you need to think about your
perception and its capacity
Maybe you need to ponder your wit
We can't all be brilliant, not all women are cute enough to be sassy
The awkward kid has grown up to be a genius
And all the normal people have gone absent

They're at the cafeteria, choosing from a prescribed menu of
unhappy

Man, I've been different from the start

Pussy has always run from me, but then again pussy aint too smart

I invented something

That something hit big

I heard the most popular guy in school works at Target

Reds a power color, I get it

Don't laugh, don't admit you get the part about the giraffe

I don't need it

I really can't take the credit for my sincere take on things, my mind
could never conceive it

But my heart knows

That there's something out there for me, I suppose

Behind the curtain of any man's humor lies his soul's prose

Is there a woman out there for me?

Only God knows

DEEP

15

What is the context for depth in your mind's reason?

When did you formulate this theory?

Tell me about that season?

I used to think my words had sway

But when I speak to my kids they just want to play

I say deep things…they hit like air

I fix my girl's sink

She then fucks me on a chair

I really enjoyed the reward for that simple action

Imma hit her with some deep truth

But in the end no satisfaction

I'm a humble soul

I mean it dammit!

I'm ahead of my time

But I really need to conquer this beer gut, on second thought I'll just

add a slice of lime

I'm watching the game, she's watching the same

The same old thing

Fix something else…and maybe it'll be the kitchen table the next time

Not the same old thing

That's deep

SUICIDE

16

The assumptions in a title

Maybe it's actually about revival

Maybe I'm just going to express a desire to live for something

Instead of act out the bum-life…and be a street king

Maybe I want to live

I know I want to give

I have a lot to share

And it's not about who cares

I just don't see the reason

For committing suicide before the child is even born

Let the child be delivered

Your idea deserves a start at least

To grow into a better world's resource

Feed someone's pain with passion and drive

Instead of focusing in…so much

Maybe you'll surprise yourself…maybe your baby will inspire you

Just maybe you will see the light at the end of the tunnel and thrive

POWER

17

From a resonant heart

Your spirit speaks mysteries

Closed wisdom is revealed as open revelation

The universe laughs at your audacity

And rewards your courageous capacity

I love speaking on deep things

Especially when I didn't know they were deep

Or when people cry at the sight of their power's reach

I love people

FAITH

18

A man of faith is a wonder to behold

A woman of faith irresistible to the touch

Faith in action overwhelming in victory over life's challenges

Faith in Love unaware of its reach and capacity

Love in knowledge is the most evolved force of wisdom the universe

holds

To love someone beyond that expression's rightful end

And endure through passionate emotion's shaky beginning

I love people

I accentuate that love through my arms reach and soul's capacity to

forgive

HOPE

19

Hope is Faith's clothing…the pair of shoes courage wears on the journey to freedom

I love people

I accentuate that love through my arms reach and soul's capacity to forgive

My heart's conviction is to see love grow in everyone and everything

I gain such strength from seeing a person resonate at the peak of their season's joy

My hope abides in the knowing that we are all one and entire in the acknowledgment of our collective heart's beat.

PEACE

20

Peace be unto you for the struggle is real

The fight long

The source of destiny's strength endless

And the soul in a man's walk true

I love people

I accentuate that love through my arms reach and soul's capacity to

forgive

My heart's conviction is to see love grow in everyone and

everything

I get such joy from seeing a person resonate at the peak of their

season's joy

My hope abides in the knowing that we are all one and entire in the

acknowledgment of our collective heart's beat.

If I were to live in that heart I would never leave

My spirit feeds it, my soul listens to it, and my mind follows the

instruction of its call

My peace is that I love the one who hates, hate the void that the

absence of love leaves, and fill the empty and despondent heart with

a renewed sense of its own purpose.

TRUTH

21

My truth frees me

Enlightens me

Abides over my life's travel and makes the path of my vision straight

and clear

So I can share my soundness with another soul's resonance

And give of the wonder I have received from the divine

I love people

I accentuate that love through my arms reach and soul's capacity to

forgive

My heart's conviction is to see love grow in everyone and

everything

I get such joy from seeing a person resonate at the peak of their

season's joy

My hope abides in the knowing that we are all one and entire in the

acknowledgment of our collective heart's beat.

If I were to live in that heart I would never leave

My spirit feeds it, my soul listens to it, and my mind follows the

instruction of its call

My peace is that I love the one who hates, hate the void that the

absence of love leaves, and fill the empty and despondent heart with

a renewed sense of its own purpose.

My truth is to define my life not through me but us

Us is the collective we that makes us all one

Nuanced through each heart's call to a specific vision

And glorified through every minds passionate act of love

Walk with strong legs

Run with a light heart

And fly into your destiny with a free spirit

That is truth manifested

RUNNING INTO TROUBLE

22

Be careful where you run to

Because there may be trouble ahead

Washboard stomachs hide a strong fist

And jelly bellies promise just that

People say they know where you're coming from

They don't…care

People claim they understand your pain

When they themselves…caused it

Take your time

Life's not a run-on sentence

Defined moments of peace, love, hope, fear, and anger

Bring a cohesion to your destiny's meaning

But some would rather run into trouble's arms of insecurity

Take the "In" out of your destiny's call

Take "Security" and house it in adventure's Ferrari

Drive faster…love harder…listen deeper…

Run…into…Love

Not trouble

TROUBLE

23

Thought we covered this already

Not in a way that defined a proper end I fear

Your destiny has more to say about it

Let's get a few more things clear

After you wake up in the morning

And realize the agenda has been set

Turn the tables on Society's vision for your future

Attack life's joy and passion without a map, attack it and don't relent

The resistance to this poem's presence is palpable

Push ahead and feel the wind…resist its chill

Your strength is resolute, you're drive unstoppable

Finish line…no that's what is expected

Do the different thing

For a new outcome

And reset the day according to Love and not hate

Let your hair grow skinhead

Let your beautiful hair show

Its blond glory

HOLD IT IN MAN

24

Hold it in man

Hold your passion in

Channel it through a funnel of love, patience, and temperament

Put the firehose down

HOW DOES THAT WORK

25

How's that working for you?

Did the instruction book get lost by itself?

Or did you hide it so the truth wouldn't be known?

You like to take credit for shit don't cha…

Maybe every new idea is a dead man's unrealized dream

Or a vibrant woman's discretionary tale

How much do you know?

About anything that matters…

How does your soul reckon with your spirit's request?

Does the sun have legs, arms, feet or rays?

And if they are rays how far do they reach?

Miles not days man, miles not days

Measured by my opinion or your knowledge's acuity?

How does anything you count on to live work?

Do you know?

AFTERLIFE

26

Afterlife is a tricky word

We talking the life after this one or no life at all

The concept of this word makes me feel very small

Because I don't get it, the truth in its resonance falls…away from me

How did this word get created?

The creator laughs right now because of its complexity… locked up

in simplicity's suit?

Man, I tire of the relevance of the search

Take "After" out and leave the meat

Life just is…whichever form that life takes on

Whether "after" or "before" just life

Stay in the present because it's the secret to the past's forgiveness…

And the future's foundation

DEATH

27

Let's attack it as a cycle…

In an ever emergent, ever-changing universe in constant motion

One state in a house of many

One resting place in a bedroom filled with slumber options

I'm done with the traditional

Its end is always static

But the truth is dynamic

Transforming yesterday's problem into today's resource or

tomorrow's blessing

Death is but a number in line waiting on a reassigned meaning and

purpose

Be ready, because life is even stranger

LOVE

28

I saw a little sea turtle leave the beach and enter the ocean's current

What a traveler I thought

All that water...so much distance in the journey for such a little tike

Fins that fit in the palm of my hand

Released from his mother's sand into the deep to survive

Sometimes the only reason God shows us an impossible situation is

so we can see the power of love in action

EMPTY

29

Empty and yet full of Power

Not possible right

Connected to a pre-determined end but then that play's script

releases from your soul's assignment and begins to live on its own...

Empty of fluid but full of air

Empty of love but full of bitterness and hate

Empty of peace but full of worry...it dissipates back into the

residence from which it came

Now that you are empty of the pain society's narrative prescribed,

you can be filled with the joy your love's expression brings

That forgotten existence was full of regret

Now only your mind's passion remains

What fills you my friend?

And what are you empty of?

PRAISE

30

Finally I get my due

At last my name can be seen

But she left you with everything

Everything is empty, you only wanted the love and joy she continues

to bring

In your heart, but never again in the body of…her mind's words

Oh my God…help me, for the power of a woman's presence during

the good times far outweighs the good times themselves

Help me because I'm going to jump out of the window of good

time's house and splat on the sidewalk of lonely days

Oh My God…help me, for the power of a women's presence far

outweighs the despondent aggression left in the wake of her

passion's absence

YOU

31

Tonight it's about you

Your body

Your mind

Your spirit

The beautiful rush of love's tide

Licking the essence off every nipple's bump

Biting your shoulder to drag you away into my cave of loving

despair

So you can fill it with hope again

As I feed on the nectar of the gods

And embrace a form so soft and supple, but full of a strength of

another kind

Bearing life inside, releasing it with a loving and reliant push

forward

Managing a man's dream before it destroys his vision to move into

its clear path

Filling you up with every inch of strength I have

Excavating your mind's passionate honey, manifested as a blanket of

exuberance

On my trunk's extended branch

LIGHT

32

Light comes through a window

Illuminates the real color of every situation faced

Black and white doesn't exist in this tapestry of human choice and nuance

Tonality must be embraced or we will all perish in a grey state of misunderstanding

When totally dark everything we bump into is undefined and therefor an impediment

The light brings clarity of vision and a true sense of directivity to our walk in this life

No wonder someone figured out a way to charge for something God... gives... us... for...FREE

ARROGANCE

33

In your heart there's a serious flaw

A leak of compassion, falling to the floor of humanity's pain

You expect humanity to lick it up like a dog licks up its vomit

I'm overwhelmed with disgust

And that's my problem…the love needs to be amplified

Not the hate

I will love instead of listen

To vitriol that poisons my vision's purpose

ANGELS

34

Angels give a wink

They spread their wings until your worries and fears shrink

Under a shroud of power, the loving hand of God's compassion

extended

When they abide over you, trouble can't see you

You and your protector have blended

Into a tapestry of dynamic and loving exchange

The stage is set for your greatness to be unfurled with each feather's

release of your talent's aim

I love angels because their destiny is set, their purpose so pure

The light that they travel and resonate in

Makes the wonder in me expand and my passion break forth with a

warm grin

Or maybe my angel is grinning at me and I'm just reflecting it

BLOCKED

35

Once again clarity eludes me

I speak but my personality's strength is lost in translation

I want to share how I feel but I'm too busy humming a foreign tune

in my mind

When did my soundtrack get stolen?

When did my soul's resonance get hijacked and replaced with a

better version

That's not mine

There's a wall around the real asshole that is me

I put it up but forgot how to take it down

It can't evolve as long as it's locked away

My goodness…all this too impress the unimpressible

DIVERSITY

36

I just had another steak sandwich from my favorite spot in town

It's so good and my tummy is so tight

But what if I ate it everyday

Same dressing for the salad

Medium rare for the succulent meat

My joyful experience would turn into dread

I'd be hyper-critical from one day to the next

Making sure my one meal was perfect

Making sure that succulent meat bled

The salad would lose its crunch

Because crunch compared to the same crunch is not crunchy

Diversity helps us to appreciate everything individually and fully

Color has more nuance, tone takes on its own life

Love takes many unique paths that gather beautiful soul's to the

same end

From the farthest beginnings

I want diversity

I want a menu that gives me a sense of my sandwich's greatness

PAIN BEFORE PLEASURE

37

Slap me once…shame on you

Slap me twice…wet panties

Slap me three times…restraining order

Slap me four times… that's a pattern

One piece of red velvet cake…damn good

Two pieces…excessive

Three pieces…glutton-ness

Four pieces…you'll never get an invite to the party again

Slap me 5 times…I'm your slave daddy and I love it

5 pieces of red velvet cake…that must be your cake!

PANDEMONIUM

38

Craziness, let's re-define it

Is it the absence of reason or too much of the same

The passion in a lover's toss of a dish across the room in anger

Or a man that won't listen to the woman he loves

A Senator who passes a law that makes dancing a crime in his

hometown

Or a dolphin that follows a shark and bites before a child loses his

life

A steak, well done

A steak not well done

A bear that chases a lion

Or a lion that won't mate with his lioness until he bite's the back of

her resistant neck

Pandemonium ensues when crazy is undefined and sane is

overinflated

Don't judge, just live in the crazy that you are…

PHASED OUT

39

I've lived my life in cycles

First it was about the moon and stars

I was enamored by their purpose

Then my guardian angel's call, and the All and Spirit's presence

Then His name was Jesus, and his Father the Almighty

But in me I saw something different…a universal voice I heard

I named Him many things but He always spoke in the same tone

I didn't like it when a name ruled out a nation

I didn't appreciate it when a name dictated my financial giving's

next move

I didn't understand it when a name gave justification for hate

So I phased out names and embraced love

I decided to name Him Sam

Silly I know

Spirit adores me

Spirit affirms me

Spirit amplifies me

I'll phase that out soon as well

Love has many names, but only one heart

One Love…One Voice…One Life…One Purpose

Us…We…Our…Universe…once phased out, now dialed in

RUSHING

40

God decided that Patience needed a brother because he was lonely

and in a rush for company

So he thought about the qualities Patience had

He said the following

"Patience is longsuffering so his brother will be short-fused"

"Patience is trusting so his brother will be cynical"

"Patience is grateful so his brother will be full of conceit"

"Patience is enduring so his brother will be short-sided"

"Patience is content so his brother will be dissatisfied"

Patience looked up to God and said, "Is my brother ready yet, I'm so

excited!"

God said, "Why in such a rush?"

Patience said, "I'm not rushing Father, just full of joy"

God smiled and said,

"That's the one good quality I'll give his brother, joy"

Joy can transform any quality it encounters because it is a bridge

from darkness to light

PRACTICAL WISDOM

41

Hard knocks on a closed doors rough experience

Petrified emotions from so many decisions gone awry

It's time for something practical and effective

Time to solidify meaning, everything goes south when you're too

subjective

We can't all be the same hero, can't all make our mark with the

same dart

Find your unique calling

So you can win from the start

So much struggle

Living in another soul's experience

Relax your mind and listen

The voice for you is far past its time of speaking

Listen to wisdom

Because it is the root from which the tree of practicality grows

And a great idea spreads its branches

Breathe deeply for a minute

Just breathe and follow that breath's intention

CAPACITY

42

In the middle of the night

My capacity calls to me

It say's "Tony live more, be more, do more"

And I wake up from a sound sleep

A vision implanted

Destiny unfurled before me like a map of the city

The obstacles in the way of my destination…not pretty

I go back to sweet slumber

Capacity calls to me

It say's "Tony love your children more, kiss and bless their feet"

And I awake from a sound sleep

A mission has its power restored in me

I see my children's pain, and their hurt is very deep

I fall back into the land of dreams temptation

Capacity calls to me

It say's "I love you Tony, why don't you feel the same way about
you?"

I don't answer…I don't wake at all

I just sleep

As I wake in the morning I look into the eyes of my capacity's sun

I say, "I've never loved me."

Capacity calls to me

It says, "Clear!!!"

And I awake from the slumber of a heart attack's call

RESONANCE

43

I can say it directly to you

Your mind would hear it

But by the time it reached your soul's residence, no volume

Muted in purpose, the message dies unclear

I could sing it to you

Full of passion and love, but by the time your soul was ready to

dance…

No rhythm, no harmony present to lead you into the divine

But if I make sure you are resonant to my destiny's tone

Then the pin-drop brings wonder, the heft of a full breath enlists a

welcome response

Even if my origin was unknown

Resonate at the frequency of your partner's heart-string played

And receive the gift of full exchange

TRANSITION

44

In the recesses of my spirit's void

There's an imperative, a powerful energy that rises

One I can't avoid

Love all and exclude none

I see the road ahead

It's littered with fake expectations, but I want a real outcome

I feel so good about so many things I don't know, can't see, but only

sense with the heart

I'm happy because I see purely

A stop along the way, two directions I see

But only one from which I should stray

Oh that my clarity could ring true right now

Transitions always challenge one's courage

Because a beam split never shines as brightly

And the power needed to complete the journey

Is locked up in the focus of the lens of who you are

Transitions…

RANDOM

45

Freedom fighting in the name of peace

For the end of peace is resident to the beginning of power's base

How can a wandering soul find this oasis of passionate community

when wandering implies a loss of way?

Digging under the earth of my flesh's society

Uprooting all dogma but I actually love dogs but wait, that aint what

I'm talkin about

Imma walk the dog and trash the dogma because the bone to be

buried is truth and he aint eating that

She said she loved me but breaking it down through actions made,

shows a lack thereof

No warranty for this bitch's failure, not a fixable offense I see

I can draw a picture of my kids when in the mood, but that mood is a

gift

Otherwise I aint

Clean something, fix something, believe in something, give your life

for something…or your love isn't real

TIRED

46

Man, the body needs rest sometimes

From the mind's prerogative

Seeing that right now, because my body's already sleeping

I still keep pushing past my body's expression

My intention is to teach it a lesson

I say when to stop

I give the orders to start

I believe in my body's capacity to honor my mind's passionate

command…

Let it emanate from my soul's prerogative…

Rooted in my spirit's universal call

HAPPY BIRTHDAY SON

47

Happy Birthday Nathaniel

What a little man you are

Peaceful spirit

Strength in quiet action

Abiding over your younger brother's mischief

Contemplating life's questions in a way only you know

What a blessing to me

Seeing you become…

I want to teach you so many things

Love you so many ways

Watch you accomplish and dream so many dreams

Kiss your first girl

Dissect your only frog

Pick a college to launch from

And give an acceptance speech for a job well done

Only Love could make a son as beautiful as you

Only faith could mold a mind into kindness and compassion as you

display

And only truth could surround your perception and fill it as you

express wonder

Happy Birthday son

RAGS TO RICHES

48

I hated my butler, he never bended to my will and taste

The sheets were the wrong color, the cuisine was a waste

Travel to places my father adored

I'm bored and overcome with apathy

My father making a deal on a vintage sword

I asked for a trip of my liking

My father found my request striking

Then I began to cry

My life so horrible

Although I couldn't find a plausible reason why

I looked to my heart

My heart said paint

I escaped through a brush with a palate so rich to choose from

Colors in nature gave me a sense of freedom

And unspoiled grandeur

"I want to paint father"

I faced his disapproving scowl

"The family business will be your home"

Now I'm relegated at night to watching the neighborhood owl

I would rather sneak away and paint the lilies in the courtyard

Sneak back and paint my father's face with every disapproving

expression

I would run away from the oppression

And became rich in joy

And poor in necessity

MASQUERADE BALL

49

The worlds a stage

I say it's more like a Ball

Costumes abound

That make short people seem tall

And lofty expectations seem small

And beautiful people seem ugly

And an awkward gate seem acceptable

Just don't go…

FEELINGS

50

Complex in application

Unnerving in expression and intensity

Bottled up or leaking out, never fully welcome

Why do we have them?

What is the purpose of the outburst, why is this vehicle optimal?

There's no right way to receive but to absorb is the key...for a man

Ignore the lies that come without context

The tears with no root don't belong in your minds exploration

Hear...absorb...relate...empathize

No other strategy given...have peace through all amplified displays

of pain's sensation

Hear...absorb...relate...empathize

And of course feel...just don't feel in front of her

Love her

BEGINNINGS

51 (Bonus)

Origins really fascinate me

I like the stories behind people's presence in their current state and

form

Ethnicity, culture, region, religion and folklore all interest my soul's

inquisitiveness

But once you're here you're here…shouldn't I accept that "here"

over all the information of "from"?

I respect the beginning and am impacted by the end

But the present should hold the most important space in my

perception

In the face of someone's beginning…

POETRY

52 (Bonus)

I have to give thanks to the power of poetry

I have been in love with its efficacy since I was a child

So many ways to express the same thought

So many facets to a young mind's literary expression

The heart of poetry is the truth of the writer's vision from the heart

I owe such a debt of gratitude for this medium's capacity

To harness my soul's affliction

If I could somehow see my pain's answer

Right in the midst of the storm's eye

Then maybe I could sit in that peace

And push out from that safe space of rest until the world-wind

subsides

Just maybe…

All these poems were written by me…in less than 24 hours. Enjoy

them and know that your capacity to express your heart, emotions,

and dreams is as endless as your imagination is set free to do so.

I wrote all 52 of these poems as a capacity exercise in less than a day. I sincerely hope that the reader has gained insight, wisdom and most of all enjoyment.

Anthony Brown

www.ingramcontent.com/pod-product-compliance
Lightning Source LLC
Chambersburg PA
CBHW072048040426
42447CB00012BB/3066